BRITAIN IN OLD PHOTOGRAPHS

THE CHANGING FACE OF LEICESTER

PAUL & YOLANDA COURTNEY

ALAN SUTTON PUBLISHING LIMITED

Alan Sutton Publishing Limited
Phoenix Mill · Far Thrupp · Stroud
Gloucestershire · GL5 2BU

First published 1995
Copyright © Paul & Yolanda Courtney, 1995

Cover photographs: front: Southgate Street,
1917; back: the Newarke before 1963.

British Library Cataloguing in Publication Data.
A catalogue record for this book is available from
the British Library.

ISBN 0-7509-1018-6

Typeset in 9/10 Sabon.
Typesetting and origination by
Alan Sutton Publishing Limited.
Printed in Great Britain by
Ebenezer Baylis, Worcester.

To John Daniell

Contents

The north side of Eastgates before the demolition of no. 6, *c.* 1890. This revealed a half-timbered structure behind (p. 28).

Leicester suffragettes in Bowling Green Street. Their banner carries the arms of Leicester but the traditional motto *Semper Eadem*, variously translated as 'always the same' or 'always itself', is replaced by a more radical message. Leicester has often combined a radical streak with provincial conservatism.

Preface

Beneath the modern city of Leicester lie four previous Leicesters that have influenced its present shape and appearance. Roman Leicester still determines much of the outline of the present core. Medieval Leicester perpetuated and adjusted the Roman legacy and left many glories behind – like the Guildhall and St Mary de Castro. Post-medieval Leicester – from broadly 1700 to 1850 – saw the definitive shift out of the Roman mould to the east and south. It was Leicester's golden period between roughly 1850 and 1920, however, that witnessed the vast expansion of housing far beyond those limits in every direction and in ways that have influenced the layout and appearance of the modern city as much as Roman Leicester dictated the essence of its medieval successor.

Of these four past Leicesters, the least known are the medieval and the post-medieval, so destructive have been the processes of later urbanization. It is therefore *only* with pictorial help that we can begin to reconstruct something of the detailed appearance of the city above ground for those periods and especially with respect to the nature of its earlier timber-framed housing, so much of which has since been lost. We are thus all peculiarly in the debt of our two learned authors, Paul and Yolanda Courtney, for researching so deeply into the drawings, prints and early photographic representations of the city; for identifying the precise views involved; and for placing them once more in some sort of identifiable context. The work and knowledge required in compiling such a collection is not to be underestimated. The result is fascinating, even uncanny, as it allows us to penetrate the mists of the intervening years to learn how familiar scenes have changed. It is a salutary reminder that cities are living organisms, not chronologically frozen elements in an artificially defined national 'heritage'.

C.V. Phythian-Adams

Introduction

This book is based on two exhibitions held at Newarke Houses Museum. The first, in 1990, was 'Discovering Newarke Houses', which marked the fiftieth anniversary of the Museum and looked at the history of Newarke Houses and its surroundings. The second exhibition, in 1993, was 'Lost Buildings of Leicester' which grew out of work on timbered buildings but extended to include the vanished buildings and streetscapes of more recent times. Both exhibitions presented the results of serious research projects to the public. Work for the exhibitions also prompted new lines of research and new discoveries. Visitors to the exhibitions provided useful information, for instance, a former textile worker helped us to date the photograph of the Fielding Johnson factory interior (p. 80).

The first section of this book aims to bring together the widespread evidence for Leicester's early stone and timber buildings in photographs, prints and paintings. It is surprising how many timber-framed buildings survived into the nineteenth and even the later twentieth century only to be demolished. Leicester is particularly fortunate in that many timbered buildings were recorded by the drawings and prints of local artist John Flower (1793–1861). Timber-framed buildings which survive today, at least fragmentarily, include Wygston's House, the former Cross Keys inn in Highcross Street, 42 Silver Street, Pearce's jewellers in the Market Place and the Angel inn in Cheapside.

Unfortunately it is difficult to reconstruct the plans or dates of many of the destroyed timber buildings. Archaeological excavation and documents suggest that a common medieval form was to have a shop at the front with a hall behind, both with chambers above on the first floor. A kitchen block often lay at the back. Leicester's timber buildings may range in date from the fourteenth to the seventeenth century. Timbers in the roof of the former Cross Keys inn, on the north side of All Saints' Church, have been dated to the fourteenth century. Many of those with curved wooden braces visible, such as the Golden Lion inn, probably date to the fifteenth or early sixteenth century. This date is suggested by comparison with surviving examples elsewhere which have been dated by tree ring analysis.

The last two sections of this book look at the landscape of central Leicester which has been radically changed even within living memory. We have concentrated on certain streets, especially in the final section, in order to convey the complex evolution of Leicester's streetscapes. Piecemeal rebuilding in wealthy Victorian Leicester swept away many old buildings. Large scale clearances for street widening date to the beginning of the century, notably the 1902 widening for the tramway. In the 1960s unprecedented destruction took place when the inner ringroad and St Nicholas Circle were constructed. This new road system reshaped many of the medieval streets of Leicester and destroyed many of Leicester's finest Georgian and Regency buildings. One suspects that 38 Southgate Street was not the only timber-framed building hidden behind a later brick frontage to have been bulldozed. We have taken the opportunity to publish many photographs taken by John Daniell, formerly of Newarke Houses Museum, to whom this book is dedicated. His photographic work is often the only surviving record of buildings demolished during the 1950s, 1960s and 1970s.

The new ringroad also cut off such historical areas as St Margaret's Church, the Newarke and the Castle from the commercial heart of the town. This contributes in no small way to the poor impressions some casual visitors to Leicester seem to take away with them. It is only thirty-two years since the town's planners wished to demolish the medieval Magazine Gateway! However, recent attempts to foster the tourism potential of 'Castle Park' bodes well for the future. The realization of the touristic and educational value of our historic monuments will help to safeguard them as well as making them more accessible to everyone. Change cannot be avoided in a living city. Nevertheless we must continue to work hard to preserve the best of our past buildings and to record those which must be replaced. Modern Leicester is a pleasant and vibrant city in which to live and work. Despite all the treasures that it has lost, few other industrial cities can boast such jewels as the Newarke and Castle Green.

The Golden Lion inn, on the corner of Highcross Street and Thornton Lane, was pulled down and rebuilt in brick in 1869. The curved braces and close studding suggest that it dates to the fifteenth or early sixteenth century. This period seems to be marked by rising standards of house construction, especially among Leicester's wealthiest residents, and a number of Leicester's buildings, such as Wygston's House, show similar features.

STONE AND TIMBER

The map (p. 10) shows the locations of a number of the buildings illustrated in this section and later in the book. It does not pretend to show a complete distribution of timber-framed houses surviving after 1800. Several such buildings came to light during work on this present book and more may yet be found lurking in old photographs or surviving behind Victorian brick façades. The apparent lack of such houses in the wealthy eastern suburb is almost certainly due to high rates of replacement building as this area became the commercial hub of the town. However, there is a concentration of timber-framed structures surviving on the four axial roads within the gates. Another factor at work here may be that housing in many of the back streets tended to be of a lower quality and was thus more likely to be rebuilt. The number of late surviving timber buildings which were inns is also noticeable.

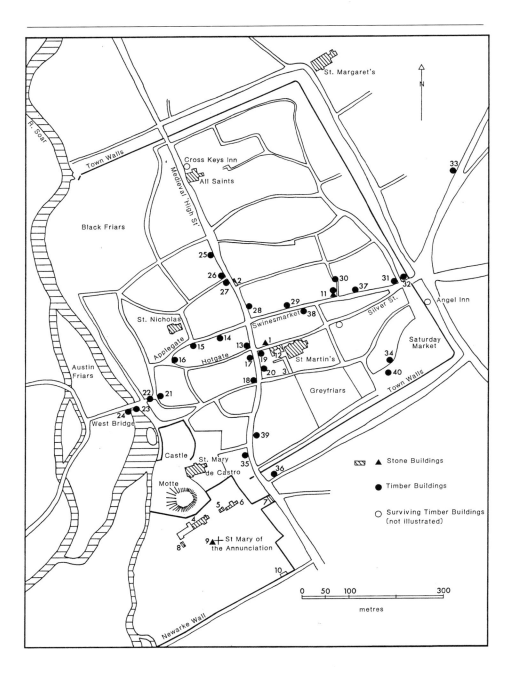

St. Margaret's

R. Soar

Town Walls

Cross Keys Inn

All Saints

Black Friars

Medieval 'High St.'

33

25

26
27
12
30
11
37
31
32

Angel Inn

St. Nicholas

28
29
Swinesmarket
38

Silver St.

Applegate

15
14
13
1

Saturday
Market

34

Austin
Friars

16
Hotgate
17
19
2
St. Martin's
40

18
20
3

Town Walls

Greyfriars

22
21

23
24
West Bridge

39

Castle

St. Mary
de Castro

35

36

Motte

Stone Buildings

Timber Buildings

Surviving Timber Buildings
(not illustrated)

5
6
7

4

9
St Mary of
the Annunciation

8

10

0   50   100   300

metres

Newarke Wall

10

Medieval Leicester: Stone and Timber Buildings

Dame Kathleen Kenyon viewing her 1936–9 excavations of the Jewry Wall site near St Nicholas Church. The dig uncovered the remains of the Roman public baths.

The Jewry Wall baths laid out for public display. This photograph was taken before the building of the adjacent archaeological museum in the early 1960s.

The undercroft or ground floor of a twelfth-century house in Guildhall (Townhall) Lane, photographed in 1861. This was recently rediscovered built into a cellar.

View by Leicester artist John Flower showing the Belgrave Gate Cross with a jettied building behind. The Cross incorporated a Roman milestone found near Thurmaston in 1771.

This jettied medieval building stood on the corner of Redcross and Highcross Streets. The half-timbered construction is largely masked by later brickwork and a stuccoed front. This building was still standing in 1922.

Lithograph by John Flower showing a house on the west side of the West Bridge. It has the date 1636 below one of its windows.

The building on the east end of the West Bridge, shown in this Flower lithograph, had been a chapel dedicated to the Virgin Mary in medieval times. After the Reformation it was used as a dwelling. The bridge and building were demolished in 1841.

John Flower published this view of Bridge Street in 1826. The jettied Royal Oak inn is on the left and the entrance to the yard of the Mitre and Keys inn can be seen at the end of the street. Both pubs were rebuilt later in the century.

Medieval timber-framed houses in Bridge Street looking towards the Mitre and Keys inn. This street was swept away by road widening in 1902 to accommodate a new tram route.

Another view of Bridge Street showing Pink's shop on the north side of the street.

Rear view of the Mitre and Keys inn, published by John Flower in 1826. The lath and plaster facing of this timbered building can be clearly seen.

Backs of timber-framed cottages in Thornton Lane.

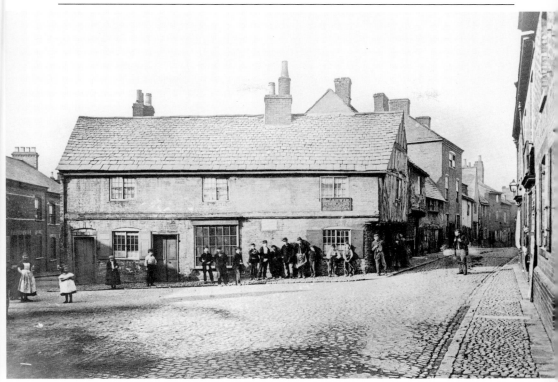

The half-timbered and jettied gable shows this brick building in St Nicholas Square to be late medieval in origin. It may have been designed as a row of shops facing the Square, though it is difficult to be sure from the altered façade. The building was demolished in around 1872. St Nicholas Street (probably part of medieval Applegate) is on the left and Thornton Lane (the medieval Hotgate) on the right.

End gable of the St Nicholas Square house and two adjacent timber-framed houses in Thornton Lane. There is no firm evidence to support the popular association of the house, which bears heraldic devices, with the parliament held in Leicester in 1414.

This 1797 drawing of the St Nicholas Square house shows the date of 1620 and several heraldic devices, some associated with the duchy of Lancaster. The date may refer to alterations rather than its original construction.

Lithograph by John Flower showing a series of half-timbered buildings in the Shambles (Applegate). It is difficult to locate this view precisely but it lies somewhere between St Nicholas Church and the West Bridge.

This half-timbered building stood opposite Holy Bones in St Nicholas Street until 1899. It was known as 'Bunyan's House' though there is no documentary evidence to support the popular belief that John Bunyan stayed here in the late seventeenth century.

Brick house on the south side of St Nicholas Street, *c.* 1890. The jetty shows that it was originally half-timbered.

No. 38 Southgate Street, photographed before its demolition in 1963. Its eighteenth-century brick frontage hid a fifteenth- or sixteenth-century timber-framed building.

The north wall of 38 Southgate Street showing the closely spaced timber studding.

The roof structure of 38 Southgate Street, photographed during demolition.

Two timber-framed buildings in Highcross Street on the south side of the Red Lion inn, 1890.

Pencil sketch of a jettied house by John Flower. The house has not been identified but was probably in Leicester.

This building, part of 96 Highcross Street, was photographed while being dismantled in 1925. It was reconstructed in the grounds of what is now Crown Hills Community College.

Sketch showing the back of the Hare and Pheasant inn in High Street, which was demolished in 1890.

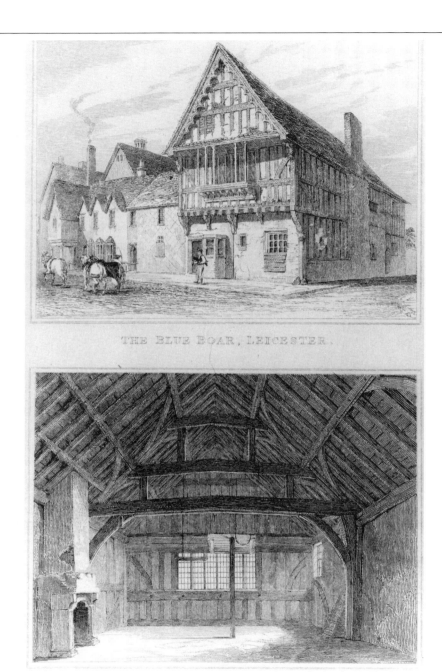

THE BLUE BOAR, LEICESTER.

Print showing the Blue Boar inn in Highcross Street and the first-floor room in which Richard III was reputed to have slept before the Battle of Bosworth in 1485. This famous fifteenth-century building was demolished in 1838.

The Admiral Rodney inn as drawn in 1850 by John Flower. This inn stood on the opposite corner to the Blue Boar inn in Highcross Street.

A nineteenth-century drawing of Highcross Street by Miss E.S. Paget showing three jettied buildings. One is the Nag's Head inn, with its distinctive porch, which was demolished in 1876. The jettied house on the left is on the corner of Redcross Street.

This timber-framed building on the north side of Eastgates was revealed in around 1890 by the demolition of a brick structure in front.

Flower's view of the timber-framed Guildhall, published in 1826. Two timber-framed buildings can be seen in the background, on the corner with Highcross Street. The building on the left corner, with decorative gables reminiscent of the Blue Boar's, is the Nag's Head inn.

The Nag's Head inn, 1864. It stood on the corner of Guildhall Lane and Highcross Street and was demolished in 1876.

Sketch by John Flower of the Nag's Head inn. A date of 1663 is shown, but the rear view in Flower's lithograph of the Guildhall suggests that the basic structure is older.

This three-storey timbered structure, probably 64 High Street, was photographed during the 1902 street widening. The front of the timber building had already been cut back, probably when the brick façade was added.

This 1864 view shows the jettied structure of Chamberlain's glove manufactory in Southgate Street, next to the Old Blue Boar hotel. The Magazine can be seen in the background.

Demolition of a timber-framed house on the corner of High Street and East Bond Street in 1903.

The sixteenth-century stone tower of Lord's Place, which had been encased in brick, was revealed during street widening in 1902. It had been part of the town house of the Earl of Huntingdon.

This timber structure, probably dating to the fifteenth century, stood at the rear of Lord's Place.

Another view of Lord's Place during demolition, showing the timber and stone parts of the building.

This Flower print looks from the Highcross down Highcross Street. In the foreground on the right are two jettied timbered houses. The house to the north of the Red Lion inn, dated 1717, also appears to have timber elements, perhaps the remnants of a jetty. The borough gaol (built 1792–3) and the Free Grammar School (built in around 1573) can also be seen.

Highcross Street in the 1950s or 1960s, looking towards the sixteenth-century Free Grammar School. The house, illustrated by Flower with a date of 1717 and standing on the north side of the Red Lion inn, still survives. On the north side of this house, the south wall of the borough gaol can still be seen in the frontage.

Detail from a print of 1745 showing a stuccoed building in the Market Place, presumably timber-framed, with sixteenth- or seventeenth-century pargetted decoration. The forked left gable is almost certainly a lithographer's error as it does not appear on another print from the same original drawing (p. 73).

The same house, drawn by Elizabeth Flower in 1839 shortly before its demolition.

The back of the Market Place house before its demolition in 1839.

Wygston's House in Highcross Street, now the Costume Museum, c. 1900. Only the hall and its chamber above survive from the medieval house. The medieval shop and chamber block on the street frontage was replaced by a brick structure in 1796.

Print by John Flower showing a range of timber-framed houses in Highcross Street on the north side of Peacock Lane. The jettied house on the corner of Redcross Street is on the right. The block of houses with rounded arches beyond Peacock Lane was built in around 1792 by John Johnson.

Timber-framed cottages in Little Lane on the north side of High Street, 1900. A reference by local historian Charles Billson suggests that these were still standing in around 1920.

Cavendish House, 1730. This mansion was built in around 1600 on the site of Leicester Abbey. King Charles I and Prince Rupert stayed here during the siege of Leicester in 1645. The house was burnt down shortly afterwards.

The south side of Cavendish House. The ruins can still be seen in Abbey Park on the north side of Leicester.

Interior view of the south wall of Cavendish House. The large window probably once gave light to a first-floor dining hall.

Wyggeston's Hospital was built in around 1515 and demolished in 1875. The three-storey end block was probably built in the eighteenth century.

The Free Grammar School in Highcross Street (built in around 1573, when it was part of a warehouse), *c.* 1950. It was badly restored in 1967 with the addition of concrete-framed windows.

The rear of the Free Grammar School as revealed by demolition in 1966.

A QUIET PRECINCT: THE NEWARKE

The Newarke or 'new work' was Henry Earl of Lancaster's foundation of a hospital to care for the elderly in 1330. His foundation was enlarged and further endowed by his son, the first Duke of Lancaster. Around 1353 work began on the Church of St Mary of the Annunciation, which was intended to serve as a mausoleum for the Lancaster dynasty. The church was described by Leland in the sixteenth century as 'not very great, but it is exceeding fair'. The church was served by a college of canons who lived in stone houses in the precinct. By the early fifteenth century the precinct was surrounded by stone walls. The Newarke Gateway (later the Magazine) probably served as guest quarters as well as being the main entrance. In 1548 the college was dissolved and the church afterwards demolished. The Newarke subsequently became a fashionable residential area for Leicester's elite, where they enjoyed exemption from borough rates until the Newarke was incorporated into the borough in 1835.

The Newarke, *c.* 1800. Trinity Hospital, largely rebuilt in 1776, is on the right. St Mary's Vicarage can be seen in the distance. Left of centre is the house built in around 1690 for Lawrence Carter on the site of the Church of St Mary of the Annunciation. The procession of women into the house is unexplained. The house became known as Shipley Ellis House after the chairman of the Midland Railway who lived there from 1853.

The Magazine Gateway and the entrance to the Militia barracks. The gateway was built in around 1400 as the main entrance into the Newarke precinct and was used as a magazine or armoury during the English Civil War. In 1682 it was purchased by the county for use by the county militia. Much of its external stonework was replaced in 1853. To the left of the Magazine is the entrance to the militia headquarters, built in the 1860s. The Magazine came close to demolition during road developments in the 1960s but was saved from the town planners to become the Museum of the Royal Leicestershire Regiment.

Timber partition on the first floor of the Magazine, photographed during its restoration in 1968. Only the main timbers now remain in place.

Two skulls found in the garderobe shaft of the Magazine, 1968. Graffiti left by prisoners shows that the Magazine was used as a prison in the late sixteenth century. The skulls may date from that period or from the Civil War but remain unexplained.

Trinity Hospital before the demolition of its far (west) end in 1898 to give access to the new Newarke Bridge. The chapel in the foreground is medieval in date but the rest of the Hospital was rebuilt in 1776.

Trinity Hospital during rebuilding in or shortly before 1901. The arches of 1776 were incorporated into the new building.

Shipley Ellis House (built *c*. 1690) in 1896 before it was incorporated into the New Art School, now the Hawthorn building of De Montfort University.

Shipley Ellis House incorporated within the structure of the Art School. It was demolished in 1932.

Another view of Shipley Ellis House showing a mixture of stone and later brickwork.

Arches of the Church of St Mary of the Annunciation were incorporated into the cellar of Shipley Ellis House in 1937 in their original position.

The church arches reconstructed in the basement of the Hawthorn building where they remain today.

The garden of Shipley Ellis House before 1896. Skeffington House, now part of Newarke Houses Museum, is in the background.

Skeffington House in 1927. The stuccoed frontage of around 1800 hides a late sixteenth-century stone building. Over the centuries the house was adapted and expanded to provide more space and privacy.

The interior of Skeffington House was gutted during restoration in 1951. The stone walls of the sixteenth-century house, now hidden by plaster, can be seen.

A fireplace photographed during the restoration of Skeffington House. Both sixteenth-century stonework and brickwork of the eighteenth century and later is visible.

A first-floor partition revealed during the restoration of Skeffington House in 1951. Originally the house was one room deep and the upper storey was reached by a single projecting staircase at the back.

The Gimson Room in Newarke Houses Museum, showing paved flooring discovered in 1957 under the present floor level.

George Shirley Harris, hosier, with his family in the garden of Skeffington House in 1867. By this time Skeffington House had been divided into two separate residences.

Another view of the Shirley Harris family in their garden in 1867. The stucco is restricted to the eastern half of Skeffington House. At the western end, by then a distinct property, various phases of stone and brickwork can be clearly seen.

Dr Jacques, who lived in Skeffington House from around 1877 to 1902, photographed alongside the tower of St Mary de Castro. The rough stonework seen in this view of the church has since been replaced.

Form 4B of Gateway Boys' School outside the front door of Skeffington House in 1934. The school opened in 1928 as a pioneering technical school and moved to its present premises on the other side of the Newarke in 1939.

The High Cross originally stood at the junction of High Street and Highcross Street. It was set up in the garden of Newarke Houses in 1952 and moved to the Market Place in 1976. This photograph shows the Lord Mayor after the unveiling ceremony in Newarke Houses garden in 1953.

Wygston's Chantry House and Rupert's Gateway (built 1423) around the turn of the century. St Mary de Castro Church is in the background.

The Chantry House after it was bombed at 10.29 pm on 19 November 1940. It was built in around 1513 by William Wygston for two chantry priests to sing masses for his soul. A third floor was later added to the building, probably in the late sixteenth century.

The Chantry House in 1957 after its restoration. This attempt to restore the building to what was thought to be its original appearance would today be regarded as vandalism.

The doorway of the Chantry House during restoration in 1953. The door was remodelled and the slab showing the arms of William Wygston, originally placed over the door of the Chantry House, was moved inside the Museum.

The back of the armorial slab showing the arms of William Wygston. When it was removed, it was discovered that it had been made from a gravestone.

Cottages in Mill Lane before their demolition in 1935 when the road was widened. The stone cottages, with later brick adaptations at the front, are of uncertain date but are presumably post-medieval. They were built into the north-east angle of the Newarke wall probably using salvaged medieval stone. In the nineteenth century they were incorporated into a courtyard with more brick cottages. Bishop Bonner's Hall (p. 60), is just out of view to the right.

A double doorway, with one side converted into a window, leading into the north side of Bishop Bonner's Hall. This building was a domestic structure of the late fourteenth or early fifteenth century, which stood astride the Newarke wall.

Fragments of a late medieval, trefoil-headed window, photographed during demolition of Bishop Bonner's Hall in 1935.

St Mary's Vicarage before its two upper storeys were removed in 1947. This late medieval building may have been the residence of the Dean of St Mary of the Annunciation. In later years it was the vicarage of St Mary de Castro and, early in the twentieth century, part of Wyggeston Girls' School.

Side view of St Mary's Vicarage before partial demolition in 1947, showing medieval stonework and later brickwork.

The Female Asylum in Asylum Street (now Gateway Street) photographed in March 1927, shortly before its demolition for street widening. It was founded in 1800 by the Revd Thomas Robinson, vicar of St Mary de Castro, to train female orphans as domestic servants.

The Newarke, *c*. 1900. On the right is the Drill Hall, with the Royal Arms over the entrance, built in 1893 for use by local volunteer forces and demolished in 1963.

The terracotta arms above the Drill Hall entrance.

The Newarke looking towards the Magazine, 1927. The view into Oxford Street has been opened up by demolition of houses on the left. The white building in the background, 'Ye Ancient Shoppe', may be another timber-framed building but it is impossible to be sure from such a small-scale view.

The Newarke looking towards the Magazine before 1963, when the militia buildings on the right were demolished. Immediately next to the medieval Magazine is the Gothic Headquarters building of 1863. In the right foreground is the Drill Hall of 1893.

Magazine Square seen from Newarke Houses garden between 1963 and 1967.

The militia houses of 1863 around the former drill square, before demolition in 1967.

The Newarke as seen from Newarke Houses in 1967. The militia square and its buildings have been swept away.

Demolition of militia buildings adjacent to the Magazine in 1963 revealed the medieval wall of the Newarke precinct. The masonry is partially hidden by later brickwork.

The south wall of the Newarke in Mill Lane viewed from the north. The Civil War gun ports and a blocked doorway can be clearly seen. This wall was the scene of some of the fiercest fighting during the Royalist siege of Leicester in 1645.

The south wall of the Newarke viewed from the corner of Fairfax Street. This and the view above date to around 1860, immediately before the wall was demolished.

A THRIVING AND PROSPEROUS TOWN

This section presents a selection of photographs illustrating life and work in Leicester, especially in the nineteenth century. The success of Leicester's hosiery industry played a major part in its Victorian and early twentieth-century prosperity. Economic success, however, led to extensive redevelopment of its historic core, sweeping away many older houses. Less obvious is the destruction to its archaeological past caused by the extensive construction of cellars along the historic street frontages of the medieval town.

Central Leicester in 1828. The town was beginning to spread to the east and south.

The Market Place. A print of 1812 from a drawing by I.C. Cockshaw, looking towards the conduit in the north-east corner of the market. There is a complete lack of timber-framed structures, and the fashionable frontages all appear to postdate 1700.

The Conduit. In 1612 Leicester was provided with a piped water system which brought water in pipes from a spring near the modern Conduit Street to the Market Place. The conduit was a hexagonal structure containing a lead tank, and it was rebuilt in 1709. In 1847 it was moved to a garden in Wigston, where this photograph was taken, having been rebuilt using new brick. The structure was finally demolished in 1960.

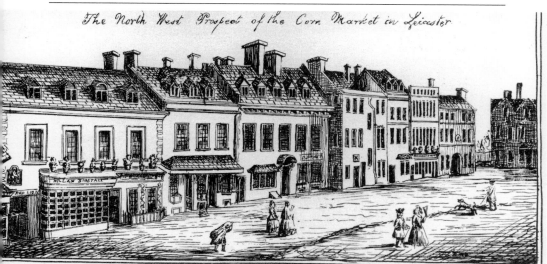

The North West Prospect of the Corn Market in Leicester.

Publish'd Ap. 9th 1745 by T: Bakewell against Birchen Lane in Cornhill & sold by M Unwin in Leicester.

The Market Place, 1745, looking towards the south-east. The fashionable façades can only be a few decades old at most.

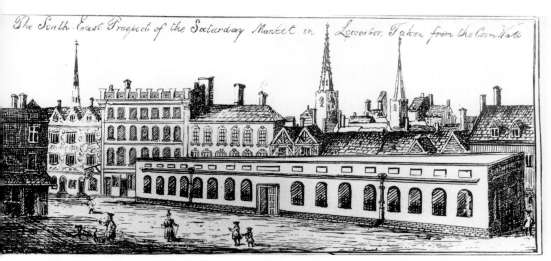

The South-East Prospect of the Saturday Market in Leicester, Taken from the Corn Walk.

The Market Place, 1742, looking towards the north-west. Behind the market building can be seen two half-timbered gables. The gabled, three-storey house on the left, with decorated plaster, was demolished in 1839.

The Market Place, 1847. The roof of the gabled building immediately behind the lamp-post dates to around 1500. It is now occupied by Pearce's jewellers.

The old Gainsborough, or old corn exchange, built in 1747–8, before its demolition in 1851 when the new corn exchange was built on the site.

The Market Place, *c.* 1852–6. The new Market Hall was built in 1851 and enlarged in 1856 with the addition of a second floor and external stairs. The statue of the Duke of Rutland was erected in 1852.

Stilton cheeses on sale in Leicester market, 1903.

Leicester market in 1902, looking north past the corn exchange.

Market stalls in 1902, looking towards the south-east corner.

The Market Place, 1914, showing Brice's saddlers and an adjacent four-storey Georgian building, long since demolished.

The Vegetable Market of 1900 in Halford Street, photographed in 1966 before its demolition in 1973. The Royal Doulton mermaids were removed to the West Bridge where they were re-erected.

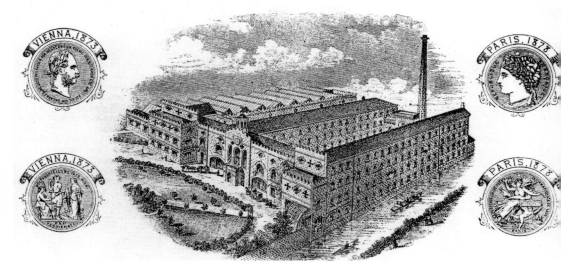

The Bow Bridge elastic webbing works in King Richard's Road, illustrated in 1891. The factory appears on a town map of 1828 as 'Kelly's factory'.

The Bow Bridge works before demolition in the 1960s. Its elaborate Gothic architecture contrasts with the plainer, more functional style of Leicester's later factories.

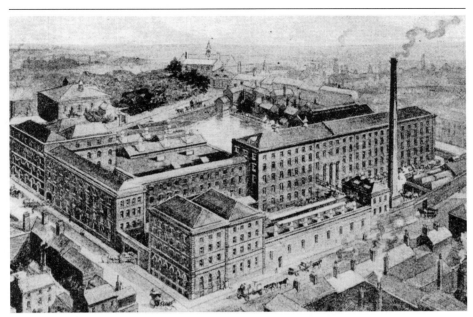

Aerial representation of the Fielding Johnson worsted factory in East Bond Street, 1891. A datestone of 1818 was recovered during demolition of the factory in the 1970s.

The derelict Fielding Johnson factory, 1971.

The reservoir inside the Fielding Johnson factory. Apparently workers sometimes swam there in hot weather.

Interior view of the Fielding Johnson factory, probably in the 1930s.

R. Morley & Sons drapery shop at 14 Cheapside. The building still survives and the Morley initials can be seen in the frontage and set into the mosaic within Morley's arcade.

The interior of Morley's, *c.* 1900. This is a rare photograph of a shop interior.

Whittaker's 'watch and clock materials and tools' department at 4 Peacock Lane. This building was demolished in around 1926.

Swain's Cheese Factor's, more recently the Antiques Complex, in Highcross Street, now St Nicholas Place. Its ceramic tile panels date to the beginning of the twentieth century.

The 'Gardener's Cottage' on the corner of Free School Lane and West Bond Street. This brick structure appears to have been built in the eighteenth or early nineteenth century incorporating an earlier stone boundary wall in its structure.

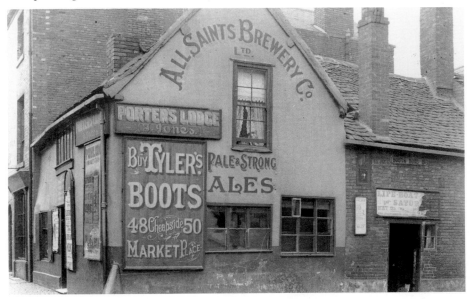

The Porter's Lodge inn, probably in the 1890s. This stood on the corner of South and East Bond Street. There is no solid evidence to confirm its reputed link with nearby Lord's Place, a sixteenth-century mansion.

Harvey Lane Baptist Chapel in 1921, just months before the chapel was destroyed by fire.

The Primitive Methodist Chapel in St Nicholas Street, 1896. This was one of many chapels lost over the years in this strongly Nonconformist town.

The house and school of Miss Mary Linwood (d. 1845) at the upper end of Belgrave Gate. The lack of symmetry in the neo-Gothic facade of around 1800 suggests two or more earlier buildings. Miss Linwood was famed locally for her needlepoint.

Rear view of 20 Applegate Street in 1922, showing a detached workshop. Such family workshops played an important role in Leicester's economy until the end of the nineteenth century.

The borough gaol in Highcross Street before demolition in 1880. It was built in 1792–3 to a design by local architect John Johnson.

The borough gaol during demolition in 1880.

The River Soar looking towards the Castle and St Mary de Castro before this section was canalized. The river was lined by willows and reed beds.

The canalization of the River Soar, *c.* 1890. This work was intended to reduce the regular winter flooding of the town. St Mary de Castro is in the background.

The Midland station, off Campbell Street, in 1856. Built in 1840, it was demolished in 1892 to be replaced by the present station on London Road.

A view from a nineteenth-century lantern slide of the Leicester and Swannington Railway station by West Bridge. The stone structure housed the station offices and was built in 1832. A new station was constructed in 1893 on a nearby site and the old buildings were later demolished.

The employment exchange, largely built of wood, which existed briefly in Applegate Street during the 1920s and early 1930s. Leicester fared better than most towns in the depression but still had its unemployed. Low cost, short-term architecture of this type can easily vanish without any record.

Horsefair Street looking towards Gallowtree Gate. The porch on the right belongs to the Three Crowns inn which was demolished in 1870. The National Provincial Bank was built on the site.

The last stage-coach leaving the Three Crowns inn in Horsefair Street in 1866. The inn is said to have been built in 1726.

Rear view of the Three Crowns inn. Its ramshackle condition suggests that it was about to be demolished.

Aerial view, taken between the 1920s and 1940s, showing the Wolsey dyeing and finishing works in north Leicester. A machinery works lies on its far side. The adjacent allotments and sports field are soon to be absorbed by the expanding factories. The terraced housing in the background dates to the 1890s.

Aerial view looking north towards Victoria Park which was created in 1866 from the old racecourse. The preservation of allotments, nursery gardens and old clay-pits in the area north of the park, as Leicester spread southwards, allowed the development of this impressive civic landscape. In the foreground is Wyggeston Girls' School, standing within its extensive playing fields, which opened on this site in 1928. Beyond are De Montfort Hall, built in 1913, and the 1923 war memorial, designed by Lutyens, at the end of a tree-lined approach.

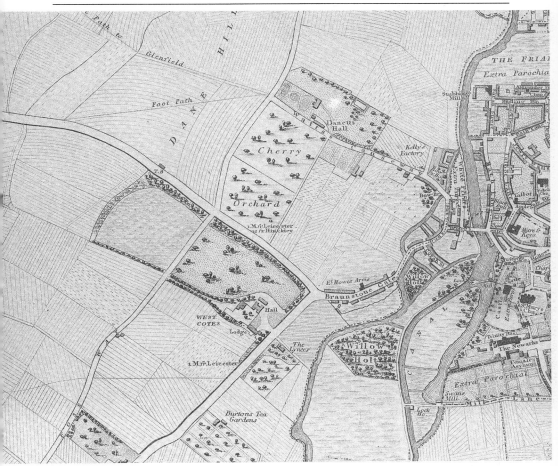

The 1828 map of Leicester showing Danet's Hall and Westcotes Grange on the west side of the town. The manor of Danet's Hall dates back to the twelfth or thirteenth century, while Westcotes was originally a farm or grange of Leicester Abbey. A moat, possibly medieval rather than a later garden feature, can be seen to the north-east of Danet's Hall. These two estates prevented the westward expansion of Leicester until the late 1800s.

Danet's Hall, showing the classical façade of the early eighteenth century. The house was demolished in 1861 after the death of its last owner, Dr Noble. Soon afterwards the estate was sold to the Leicester Freehold Land Society and terraced housing was built on the site.

This wall painting was discovered in a house in Loseby Lane in the 1960s and appears to show Danet's Hall in the early or mid-eighteenth century when it had Palladian wings and a formal garden.

Danet's Hall in 1789, showing how the house had been adapted according to the fashion of the day, with the loss of the Palladian wings and an informal garden.

Westcotes in 1798 with its classical façade of around 1730 and an informal garden intended to imitate nature.

Rear of Westcotes Grange before its demolition in 1886. Mrs Fielding Johnson, writing in the late nineteenth century, suggested that the back of the house included medieval work, though this is not very evident from the photograph.

LEICESTER STREETSCAPES

This section shows a variety of streetscapes in central Leicester which have since been transformed by road-widening or general redevelopment. The earliest recorded large-scale planned demolition was the destruction of the south suburb by the parliamentarian defenders of Leicester in 1645 in order to shorten the town's defences. Its post-Civil War redevelopment, however, was slow and piecemeal.

Twentieth-century redevelopment has been spectacular, commencing at the end of 1901 when the borough council took over the Leicester Tram Company with the aim of introducing electrification, one of many major civil engineering schemes the borough undertook around the turn of the century. In 1902 the street widening necessary for a new tram route to run along the High Street and over the Soar destroyed many buildings in the heart of Leicester. The frontages, though rarely interiors or backyards, of many of these buildings are preserved in photographs. Other street widening schemes followed, for instance, along the east side of Belgrave Gate in 1930. Most devastating, however, was the inner ringroad scheme of 1963 which totally swept away the medieval street pattern of the western part of Leicester.

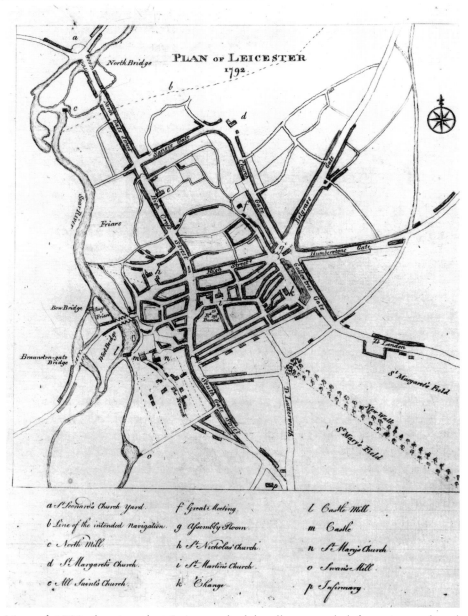

PLAN OF LEICESTER
1792

a *St Leonard's Church Yard*	f *Great Meeting*	l *Castle Mill*
b *Line of the intended Navigation*	g *Assembly Room*	m *Castle*
c *North Mill*	h *St Nicholas' Church*	n *St Mary's Church*
d *St Margaret's Church*	i *St Martin's Church*	o *Swan's Mill*
e *All Saint's Church*	k *Change*	p *Infirmary*

Map of 1792 showing that Leicester had hardly expanded from its medieval boundaries. The tree-lined Queen's or New Walk leading to the racecourse on what is now Victoria Park, was laid out in 1785.

View of west Leicester in 1836. An enclosure act in 1804 soon allowed the town to spread southward. The crenellated Gothic architecture of the new county gaol of 1825–8 is very noticeable, as are the growing number of factory chimneys.

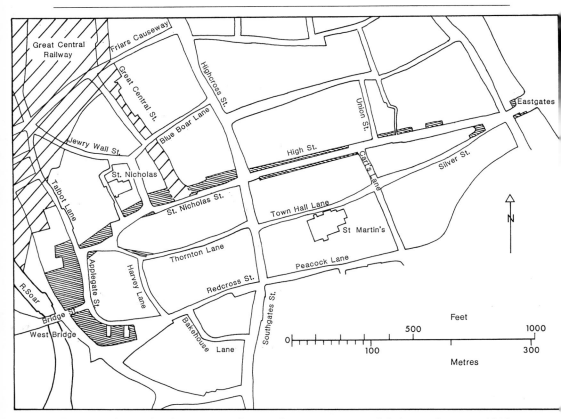

This map shows the destruction of street frontages in central Leicester between 1888 and 1904. The wide hatching indicates destruction caused by the construction of the Great Central Railway during 1896–8. The smaller hatching shows other road widening, mostly carried out in 1902 for the new tram route down High Street and across the West Bridge. However, a few small areas may have resulted from other redevelopment; for example, the building on the north side of Eastgates was demolished around 1890.

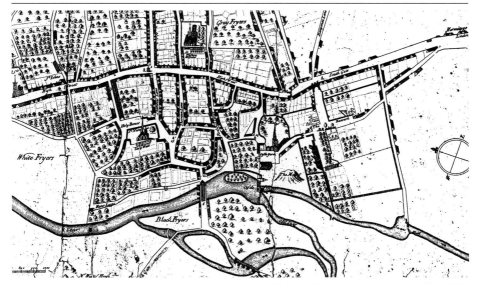

Part of John Robert's town map of 1741 showing the medieval streets to the west of the medieval High Street (later Highcross and Southgate Streets).

This 1967 photograph shows the destruction of the western part of the medieval town brought about by the construction of St Nicholas Circle: (A) St Nicholas and Jewry Wall; (B) Wygston's House; (C) the Magazine.

One of a series of views taken from St Martin's steeple in 1867, looking north-west: (A) the Magazine; (B) Wyggeston's School; (C) St Mary de Castro.

A northward view from St Martin's: (A) Golden Lion inn on the corner of Highcross Street and Thornton Lane; (B) St Nicholas.

An eastward view from St Martin's: (A) Lord's Place on the High Street; (B) Fielding Johnson factory.

A westward view from St Martin's: (A) Alderman Newton's school; (B) New Street.

The Duke of York pub on the corner of Millstone Lane and Southgates in 1928. A timber-framed structure can just be seen at the back of the pub in Millstone Lane.

View looking south down Southgate Street in 1917. The Magazine is on the right.

A view down Southgates towards the high tower of Everard's brewery in the interwar years.

No. 14 Oxford Street photographed in 1909. This building was built in 1771 and stood on the corner of Newarke Street and Southgate Street. It was demolished by road widening in 1926.

The same building from the south in 1909. Allen House now stands on the site.

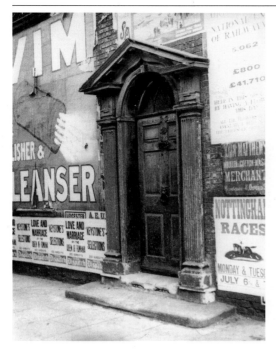

The doorway of 14 Oxford Street in 1925.

The door knocker of 14 Oxford Street in 1925.

Southgate Street in 1922 looking north. The houses with rounded arches on the right were built by local architect John Johnson in around 1792.

Southgate Street in 1922, looking south. The jettied building on the right is on the corner of Redcross Street.

These houses in Southgate Street were built in around 1792 by the architect John Johnson on the site of his birth. Behind them stands Johnson's Consanguinitarium, built to house his poor relatives.

Southgate Street before demolition work in 1965. The hosiery factory, dated 1897, is on the south corner of Redcross Street. The high tower of Everard's brewery is in the background.

Everard's brewery and adjacent houses on the west side of Southgate Street in 1962.
The three houses each had a brick at the rear bearing the date 1824.

Detail of shopfront by Everard's brewery.

The Blue Boar Hotel on the west side of Southgate Street, photographed in 1967 during work on the underpass. It was finally demolished in 1971.

Nos 17–23 Oxford Street, a block of eighteenth- and early nineteenth-century houses, awaiting demolition in 1963.

Houses in Southgate Street, opposite Bakehouse Lane, said to date from the eighteenth century. They were awaiting demolition in 1965. St Martin's Church can be seen in the background.

Southgates underpass during construction in 1967.

Early nineteenth-century houses, in the Grecian style, in Asylum Street (now Gateway Street), photographed shortly before demolition in 1957.

Grecian-style houses, probably of the early nineteenth century, which stood on the corner of Highcross Street and Causeway Lane, and were demolished in 1957.

High Street in 1876 viewed from the Highcross Street junction, with Hallam's hardware store on the right and a temperance establishment on the left.

Hallam's store on the corner of High Street and Highcross Street, probably photographed in 1903 shortly before demolition and rebuilding. William Hallam was a general dealer who traded under the slogan 'the family frypan'.

High Street, looking east from Cart's Lane towards Lord's Place (Huntingdon's Tower), *c.* 1900. The stone tower of Lord's Place, originally one of a pair, survived from the sixteenth century encased in eighteenth-century brick.

Shops on the north side of High Street, probably shortly before the street widening of 1902. No. 31 is clearly a jettied structure of timber-framed construction.

Payne's fish and game shop in High Street, shortly before demolition in 1902. Notice the open display of meat and the hooks for hanging game. This building probably dates to the late eighteenth or early nineteenth century.

A Georgian house dated 1794 in the High Street, photographed a hundred years later in 1894.

St Nicholas Street. The large shop to the left of Cyril Noon's is Dryad's furniture store. This area was demolished in 1963 for the construction of St Nicholas Circle and the inner ringroad.

Dryad's in St Nicholas Street. The bunting and Royal Arms suggest that this photograph was taken in 1953, Coronation year.

Pentonville, a cul-de-sac off Grange Lane, shortly before demolition in 1957. This street was built about 1862. It was apparently intended originally to provide two-storey workshops but by this century had become slum housing.

A backyard with toilet block in Pentonville, *c.* 1957.

New Pingle Street in 1957, shortly before demolition of this area.

The Pingle Street area in 1957, awaiting demolition.

A shared backyard, Pingle Street area, 1957.

The Newarke Tavern in Mill Lane before demolition in around 1960.

The White Hart Hotel in the Haymarket, *c.* 1958–60. This hotel had been rebuilt at the beginning of the century and was demolished in 1961, making way eventually for the Haymarket Centre.

The Stag & Pheasant Hotel in Humberstone Gate, *c.* 1958–60. This had been rebuilt in 1905 and was demolished in 1961, as part of the same development as the White Hart site.

Orton's basketworks at 6 Churchgate, *c.* 1900. The manufactory and shop existed alongside each other. The goods display is typical of the period.

Nos 93–97 Churchgate (eastern side) in the 1930s. Victorian shop fittings of this type have now almost entirely been swept away.

Belgrave Gate in 1930, looking from the cross at the junction with Bedford Street towards Belgrave, before extensive road widening along its eastern side.

A view from Belgrave Gate Cross towards Bedford Street in 1930, before road widening.

Shops, and entrance to a court, in Belgrave Gate in the 1920s. These buildings between Narrow and Wilton Streets were demolished for road widening in 1930.

Belgrave Gate looking towards the clock tower in 1930 before the eastern side of the street was demolished.

Nos 247–259A Belgrave Gate between Britannia Street and Melton Street in the 1920s before demolition in 1930.

No. 53 Belgrave Gate, on the corner of Hill Street, in the 1920s. This fine Georgian house, formerly used by William Colton and Sons as a rope and twine manufactory, appears to have been abandoned by 1928.

Acknowledgements

This book is based on negatives, photographs and prints held by Leicestershire Museums Arts and Records Service. We particularly wish to thank Professor C.V. Phythian-Adams for writing the preface and Catherine Lines for her hard work copying photographs. Steph Mastoris, Julia Collieu, Peter Foster, Richard Buckley, John Lucas, Stuart Warburton, David Smith, Robin Jenkins and Hilda Stoddart all provided further assistance or information. Copyprints of most of the photographs in this volume are available from Leicestershire Museums Service. Enquiries may be made to Leicestershire County Record Office, Long Street, Wigston, Leicestershire or to Newarke Houses Museum, The Newarke, Leicester LE2 7BY.

The Newarke bridge was constructed in 1898 to link the Newarke to the west bank of the River Soar. The west end of Trinity Hospital had to be demolished to give access, but in 1901 the hospital was extensively rebuilt.

BRITAIN IN OLD PHOTOGRAPHS

To order any of these titles please telephone Littlehampton Book Services on 01903 721596

Scunthorpe, *D Taylor*
Skegness, *W Kime*
Around Skegness, *W Kime*

LONDON

Balham and Tooting, *P Loobey*
Crystal Palace, Penge & Anerley, *M Scott*
Greenwich and Woolwich, *K Clark*
Hackney: A Second Selection, *D Mander*
Lewisham and Deptford, *J Coulter*
Lewisham and Deptford: A Second Selection, *J Coulter*
Streatham, *P Loobey*
Around Whetstone and North Finchley, *J Heathfield*
Woolwich, *B Evans*

MONMOUTHSHIRE

Chepstow and the River Wye, *A Rainsbury*
Monmouth and the River Wye, *Monmouth Museum*

NORFOLK

Great Yarmouth, *M Teun*
Norwich, *M Colman*
Wymondham and Attleborough, *P Yaxley*

NORTHAMPTONSHIRE

Around Stony Stratford, *A Lambert*

NOTTINGHAMSHIRE

Arnold and Bestwood, *M Spick*
Arnold and Bestwood: A Second Selection, *M Spick*
Changing Face of Nottingham, *G Oldfield*
Mansfield, *Old Mansfield Society*
Around Newark, *T Warner*
Nottingham: 1944–1974, *D Whitworth*
Sherwood Forest, *D Ottewell*
Victorian Nottingham, *M Payne*

OXFORDSHIRE

Around Abingdon, *P Horn*
Banburyshire, *M Barnett & S Gosling*
Burford, *A Jewell*
Around Didcot and the Hagbournes, *B Lingham*
Garsington, *M Gunther*
Around Henley-on-Thames, *S Ellis*
Oxford: The University, *J Rhodes*
Thame to Watlington, *N Hood*
Around Wallingford, *D Beasley*
Witney, *T Worley*
Around Witney, *C Mitchell*
Witney District, *T Worley*
Around Woodstock, *J Bond*

POWYS

Brecon, *Brecknock Museum*
Welshpool, *E Bredsdorff*

SHROPSHIRE

Shrewsbury, *D Trumper*
Whitchurch to Market Drayton, *M Morris*

SOMERSET

Bath, *J Hudson*
Bridgwater and the River Parrett, *R Fitzhugh*
Bristol, *D Moorcroft & N Campbell-Sharp*
Changing Face of Keynsham,
  B Lowe & M Whitehead

Chard and Ilminster, *G Gosling & F Huddy*
Crewkerne and the Ham Stone Villages,
  G Gosling & F Huddy
Around Keynsham and Saltford, *B Lowe & T Brown*
Midsomer Norton and Radstock, *C Howell*
Somerton, Ilchester and Langport, *G Gosling & F Huddy*
Taunton, *N Chipchase*
Around Taunton, *N Chipchase*
Wells, *C Howell*
Weston-Super-Mare, *S Poole*
Around Weston-Super-Mare, *S Poole*
West Somerset Villages, *K Houghton & L Thomas*

STAFFORDSHIRE

Aldridge, *J Farrow*
Bilston, *E Rees*
Black Country Transport: Aviation, *A Brew*
Around Burton upon Trent, *G Sowerby & R Farman*
Bushbury, *A Chatwin, M Mills & E Rees*
Around Cannock, *M Mills & S Belcher*
Around Leek, *R Poole*
Lichfield, *H Clayton & K Simmons*
Around Pattingham and Wombourne, *M Griffiths,*
  P Leigh & M Mills
Around Rugeley, *T Randall & J Anslow*
Smethwick, *J Maddison*
Stafford, *J Anslow & T Randall*
Around Stafford, *J Anslow & T Randall*
Stoke-on-Trent, *I Lawley*
Around Tamworth, *R Sulima*
Around Tettenhall and Codsall, *M Mills*
Tipton, Wednesbury and Darlaston, *R Pearson*
Walsall, *D Gilbert & M Lewis*
Wednesbury, *I Bott*
West Bromwich, *R Pearson*

SUFFOLK

Ipswich: A Second Selection, *D Kindred*
Around Ipswich, *D Kindred*
Around Mildenhall, *C Dring*
Southwold to Aldeburgh, *H Phelps*
Around Woodbridge, *H Phelps*

SURREY

Cheam and Belmont, *P Berry*
Croydon, *S Bligh*
Dorking and District, *K Harding*
Around Dorking, *A Jackson*
Around Epsom, *P Berry*
Farnham: A Second Selection, *J Parratt*
Around Haslemere and Hindhead, *T Winter & G Collyer*
Richmond, *Richmond Local History Society*
Sutton, *P Berry*

SUSSEX

Arundel and the Arun Valley, *J Godfrey*
Bishopstone and Seaford, *P Pople & P Berry*
Brighton and Hove, *J Middleton*
Brighton and Hove: A Second Selection, *J Middleton*
Around Crawley, *M Goldsmith*
Hastings, *P Haines*
Hastings: A Second Selection, *P Haines*
Around Haywards Heath, *J Middleton*
Around Heathfield, *A Gillet & B Russell*
Around Heathfield: A Second Selection,
  A Gillet & B Russell
High Weald, *B Harwood*
High Weald: A Second Selection, *B Harwood*
Horsham and District, *T Wales*

Lewes, *J Middleton*
RAF Tangmere, *A Saunders*
Around Rye, *A Dickinson*
Around Worthing, *S White*

WARWICKSHIRE

Along the Avon from Stratford to Tewkesbury, *J Jeremiah*
Bedworth, *J Burton*
Coventry, *D McGrory*
Around Coventry, *D McGrory*
Nuneaton, *S Clews & S Vaughan*
Around Royal Leamington Spa, *J Cameron*
Around Royal Leamington Spa: A Second Selection,
  J Cameron
Around Warwick, *R Booth*

WESTMORLAND

Eden Valley, *J Marsh*
Kendal, *M & P Duff*
South Westmorland Villages, *J Marsh*
Westmorland Lakes, *J Marsh*

WILTSHIRE

Around Amesbury, *P Daniels*
Chippenham and Lacock, *A Wilson & M Wilson*
Around Corsham and Box, *A Wilson & M Wilson*
Around Devizes, *D Buxton*
Around Highworth, *G Tanner*
Around Highworth and Faringdon, *G Tanner*
Around Malmesbury, *A Wilson*
Marlborough: A Second Selection, *P Colman*
Around Melksham,
  Melksham and District Historical Association
Nadder Valley, *R. Sawyer*
Salisbury, *P Saunders*
Salisbury: A Second Selection, *P Daniels*
Salisbury: A Third Selection, *P Daniels*
Around Salisbury, *P Daniels*
Swindon: A Third Selection, *The Swindon Society*
Swindon: A Fourth Selection, *The Swindon Society*
Trowbridge, *M Marshman*
Around Wilton, *P Daniels*
Around Wootton Bassett, Cricklade and Purton, *T Sharp*

WORCESTERSHIRE

Evesham to Bredon, *F Archer*
Around Malvern, *K Smith*
Around Pershore, *M Dowty*
Redditch and the Needle District, *R Saunders*
Redditch: A Second Selection, *R Saunders*
Around Tenbury Wells, *D Green*
Worcester, *M Dowty*
Around Worcester, *R Jones*
Worcester in a Day, *M Dowty*
Worcestershire at Work, *R Jones*

YORKSHIRE

Huddersfield: A Second Selection, *H Wheeler*
Huddersfield: A Third Selection, *H Wheeler*
Leeds Road and Rail, *R Vickers*
Pontefract, *R van Riel*
Scarborough, *D Coggins*
Scarborough's War Years, *R Percy*
Skipton and the Dales, *Friends of the Craven Museum*
Around Skipton-in-Craven, *Friends of the Craven Museum*
Yorkshire Wolds, *I & M Sumner*